TRUTH

TRUTH

Spiritual Inspirations and Teaching

—m—

TRACY HARRIS

authorHOUSE

AuthorHouse™
1663 Liberty Drive
Bloomington, IN 47403
www.authorhouse.com
Phone: 833-262-8899

Published by AuthorHouse 11/11/2022

ISBN: 978-1-4685-4811-2 (sc)
ISBN: 978-1-4685-4812-9 (e)

Library of Congress Control Number: 2012901701

Print information available on the last page.

Any people depicted in stock imagery provided by Thinkstock are models, and such images are being used for illustrative purposes only.
Certain stock imagery © Thinkstock.

This book is printed on acid-free paper.

TABLE OF CONTENTS

INTRODUCTION

I believe that you are the Son of God and you died & rose on the third day. I ask that you come into my life, save me from my sins and make me whole. I confess that Jesus is Lord. I accept you as Lord and savior over my life.

Now according to Romans 10:9. "If you confess with your mouth that Jesus is Lord and believe in your heart that God raised Him from the dead, you will be saved." "I am saved". Now Lord I ask you to led me to a faith based bible believing, Teaching & Preaching Holy Ghost Filled Church that I may grow in the grace of God.AMEN!!!

TO JESUS

Lord as I re-issue this book into publication, I want to thank you in advance for all of your marvels works. I am just, so grateful for where I've been and what I've seen. Thank you for where I'm going and for your wonderful GIFT OF GRACE.

As Pastor Winans preached it May 6, 2012, it is but by grace that we are saved. Thank you for covering me. Thank you! I will be sure to express mercy mingled with compassion towards others as I continue this journey, in the matchless name of Jesus.

GRATITUDE

First to Lady Bug and Mommie (Amia and A Laya) my grand children whom I love. Secondly, to my son & daughter Mesha Brown & De Anthony Harris my two adult children. I love you both, but God got ya. Walk in his guidance and continue to follow him always. You have brought me many laughs and much joy.

I thank my mother Marinda Louise Harris (I love you) you were a blessing all by yourself. Special thanks go out to Larry Weathersby & Shannon Gardner for their assistance with Lilly and the Angel. Special thanks go out to Love Design for the photography for both Lilly and the Angel and Truth. Thanks Iesha.

PRAYER

Lord I believe that you died and rose on the third day. I believe that you are the son of God. I'm asking that you come into my life and heal my soul, deliver me and make me whole. Strengthen me with your love and guide me through my future decisions. Change my life course and deliver my soul from the path of destruction. Amen!

RETURN

Return to me for I can see that your heart has turned from me. Return you see for I still love thee. My peace is yours if you will embrace it in truth again. Believe in and follow me. Trust in me and you will see that my words I speak are truth in life they will set you free. Return, to me for my joy is calm and my love true. No longer will you have to live simply existing in a dim reality of gloom and, doom.

My council is real and my deliverance is free. All I ask is that you return to me. You will come to see that my love endures the test of time and my faithfulness in no other will you find. My proof of commitment is true. If only you would return to me.

Oh! Come and see that true love is mine. With my arms stretched wide all I ask if that you'll come once again and be mine. My arms await your sweet embrace. My child your sins are not too great. "Come, embrace your faith and return to me saith the Lord.

RELIGIOUS

I sit at home in my holy state pretending to keep the faith. I know of the truth, but I refuse to shake this oh, so familiar state. The preacher has said that I must come to church, yet I still say that I don't have to fellowship with those hypocrites. I see them now and I see them live and still I say I do not have to strive with them in order to live. You see my mother, her mother and my great great granny have said it too that it is not important to fellowship with you.

They have lived this way for centuries you see. My entire family have set a pattern for me. Tell me why should I come and why should I stay when my family has trained me to live this way. You speak of this holiness and how I must be clean. Tell me where is it required of me to live this way. My mother drank and my father did too, but yet they believed and were saved too. You say no sex for me this can't be true. Because, my man is my life. I told you once and I'll tell you again my family did it and it worked for them. What worked, so well for them is swell for me; because, at their funeral the preacher said that they went to heaven you see.

That is why I don't believe in what you say. There have been paths set before me you see. I was told once saved always saved. They never said otherwise, so you tell me just why should I believe? To die in sin means to be hell bound. Being a religious person will seal you down. There is no life in fleshly things. There is no life in having a religious demon bring you fleshly fame.

The ways before you are paths of sin. To continue there will total in the wages of sin. The traditions of life that we learn early and therein are not always the ways of true life that Jesus has planned. He has set a way that will guarantee us true fame. To be heaven bound is his greatest plan. You must fellowship this is true. That is the only way that your love will blossom and grow within you. Believe in change and you will see that the life you live is only in vain. Being able to love and forgive others of their sins and to be able to deal with others and their personalities will challenge you. This is when love will see you through (not your love for your love is very limited compared to the love of Jesus Christ).

Therefore, follow through with the will and the plan of Christ. Jesus was tried multiple times by the jews, but his love prevailed. Know the truth and accept change; because, you can not grow alone at home. This is not Jesus plan for you. Don't make excuses about others sins ;because, it is they that will be judged for their sins and not you. However, you are accountable for your own actions and sins so stay free and live in liberty.

I am Ashamed

Look at me I was standing you see. I was once a debater of the word you see. I could tell you of the life of Christ and I could even persuade you to follow me. I walked with Christ for a few years, I believe. I talked the talk and I walked the walk, but I did not stop to look and see that my life with Christ was in danger you see. I was in danger to my old man you see. I was too blind to see that my old ways were still in control and not the new me you see. I believed my self to be very strong in Christ you see. Oh! how flesh can deceive. For it deceive a foolish soul like me. I was in my flesh all the while and I really didn't see that I was going down the wrong road you see. I saw the signs, but I ignored the yearning of my inner man.

Looking back I still remember just how good Jesus had been to me. I remember his loving grace, and his tender mercies, and how he applied them to me. As I pass by in the memory of my mind I can still find a little grain of peace within me. Desiring to come back to Christ and to church, but the shame of others knowing that I have fallen well it had overtaken me. The shame of others knowing that I am the one that thought themselves to be standing ever so, tall has fallen from grace. You know my image was my everything.

As I lay wounded, unable and paralyzed from Gods grace and bound in my sin truly desiring to come back in, satan my task master is riding me and he knows that I am weak. No matter it is deliverance that I seek. In a moments time I remembered this time that it is Jesus who delivered me. In the blinking of the enemies eye you see I fail to my knees and I called on the name of Jesus and just like that, I feel the yoke of bondage breaking off of me. The weights of my sins are quickly leaving me; because, the anointing is present and all over me. For it is destroying the yokes that have, so easily over taken me.

I'M FREE, can't you see the tears of deliverance falling from me? Can't you see the sweet peace of deliverance over taking me? I'M FREE, I can't stop saying those words. I had been bound for so, long you see. Won't you at least rejoice with me. Don't remember the when just be glad for me now. Don't remember my sins for in Christ I am no longer bound. For the grace of liberty has finally reclaimed me. I am no longer ashamed;because, his loving arms are all around.

Stop Looking At Man

Many Christians have looked to man for many reasons and for many seasons. Man has become a dependency to them. They look to him as a deliverer, as a healer, and as a favor giver. There are times when we look to our pastor for favor. We look for them to call out our name only to obtain that moment of fame. Many saints only acknowledge those that are called out by the leader in the mist of the congregation.

Well your redeemer is not man nor is it of man. It is of God and by God. Many saints fall; because, they are looking at man. Let me explain man to you. Man is a vessel that is willing to be used by God. His total surrenderance is to God. His honor is from God ;because, of his life that he has lost only to gain eternal life. Just a reminder this life did not come cheap. Even though it seems, so pleasant and swell. Don't forget that he has gained his fame from heavens rain. He is a broken shell. Broken to his will and his zeal. He has been redeemed by his mender "Jesus." Jesus is the honor giver, Jesus is the healer, Jesus is his deliverer. The honor of course he gives back to the honoree, which is "Jesus." He receives no honor that is not his. He will lay no claim to healing you so, why then will you?

It is all by the spirit of God. The yolk breaking anointing that has been promised to you. Stop looking at man. Oh! how deceived are we for we have replaced the spirit of God and the glory of God with man. Yes! God has set all things in order throughout the body of Christ. It is not the will of God that we replace him with man. If you continue in this path you will eventually tread in a dangerous place. The healing, deliverance, and the miracles is all within the power of God and by the spirit of God. Know where your help comes from. Your redeemer is Jesus and not man. Only Jesus can get you to the father, who is the creator of life your life none the less. Rest on him and in him. Stop looking at man and give him the honor that Jesus has given him and not God's honor. Stop looking at man.

CLEAN

The Old Testament is a shadow of things to come. Before Jesus the people purchased different animals for different sacrifices. For a sin offering they brought a young bullock without a spot or blemish (Leviticus 4:3), for a peace offering they offered it of a herd (Leviticus 3:1), and for a trespass they offered a ram with shekels of silver (Leviticus 5:15). Being a chose generation a royal priest hood we stand before the people and in most cases we take the people before God. No not in the sense that they confess their sins to us, but through prayer we take them into heavenly places. In doing, so we should make sure that they are cleansed without spot and blemish before presenting them before the king.

Jesus even gave us instructions in Matthew 6: 9-15. Romans 4:4 speaks of debts as being metaphorically of sin as a debt. As we stand before God we ought to be sure to remit or retain the sins of the people. Not to mention asking God's forgiveness for them, too often we pray and we take the filth of ours and and others of which we pray before God. How then do we really honor and reverence our God if we dishonor him with the same thing he hates which is sin?

Even in alter call we should do likewise seeing that every sin that is committed is committed without the body (I Corinthians 6:18). For all that come to the alter may not all be beleivers at first. Therefore, the remitting or their sins is essential in that they may receive the fullness of their deliverance. Also, having their sins will give them more clarity before prayer, so that they can truly receive and all prophecies from the Father with understanding during prayer, so that they will not be focusing in on their sins, while you are praying for them.

After prayer, so that they can be free of any guilt or shame;because, it is a mind game that the enemy does to make one think that they are playing with God. Therefore telling them that they are bigger sinners, or a liar of even Unworthy of Gods love and grace. As Christians we are to set the example for others coming into the faith. If we don't remit sins how then do we expect those coming in to do likewise?

I'm Hurting Can You Tell?

I'm hurting can you tell? Yet, so close to me but still so far. Can you see the wound that is deep within me? Can you feel the loneliness that is there? I'm hurting can you tell?

Can you soothe the pain? Can you comfort me? Are you looking closely or are you glancing at me? I'm hurting can you tell. So, many Christians are hurting, so many wounds go unhealed, so many tears unrvealed. I'm hurting can you tell?

It's time to walk in love and in the spirit. Look! open your eyes and see. See! the pain that's within me. Love me pass my fault and pass my sins. Love me not judge me. Love me and allow the Christ in you to rush in.

There is someone that God has placed in your life to nurse with love, patience, long-suffering and joy, but you ignore their hurts.

Allow the Christ in you to minister to those hurts and to those lost souls. To restore and renew the weak and fainthearted. You have a calling and your ministry isn't on the pulpit. Just look around there are so, many babes in Christ who need to be held spiritually and nursed, but your life you know it just has to be right.

Their hurting while your waiting for a door to open behind the stand. Jesus has opened up several door's around you. Your neighbors, your family, your CO-workers and friends.Can't you hear with your spiritual ear I'm hurting, I'm hurting can't you tell.

Jesus has appointed you what are you going to do? Look their hurting soothe that hurt with prayer and love. Nurse them in the spirit. I'm hurting can you tell? Listen to your spirit Hear the voice of God minister the word of life to you for them.

There is such great joy in giving life and renewing a persons spirit and in encouraging them.Move by the spirit and minister peace and love. The people that are surrounding you love not hate (inspite of what they have did or said to you) love not spite and watch your spirit.Rejoice and become revived.Listen I'm hurting can you tell?

DROUGHT

What is this? I can't hear. The word of God has fallen from my ears. My barrels are dry and lighting has fallen from my eyes. Behold no rain has fallen from the sky. My peace you know I seek, but it is far from me. My life he did seek, but I hide it deep in my stink, while he did seek for it even in the depth of my stink I ran from him; because you see my stink was not stunk to me. Now low he holds the rain; because, I did seek the wrong form of fame. I sought the witches and those easy get rich claims. I went my own way; because, his way seemed too hard for me. And low in the tail of my end there is no more fame and no more rain. For Jesus holds it while I wonder through the depth of my stink.

Well the rain is the word of the truth which was wasted in time by you. The word he has refrained; because, with your life you have brought much shame to his name If only you would REPENT. Then and only then would he release the rain while you are still in your stains, and the drought would come to an end. For without the rain there is no fame only shame.

I'm Searching

I have a question for you. Have you ever seen a man searching for anything? Have you ever seen the face of distress? Have you ever seen a soul in search of being made whole? If you could see me you would finally see the face of all three abiding and living within me. For I go from day to day seeking to be free. I roam from house to house looking for deliverance you see, looking hear and searching there.

I sat in church today, but a change has not yet come my way I went to Sunday School too, but guess what the anointing did not flow through. I went to bible study and my deliverance did not come to set me free. Where can I go and what must I do? I have a request for the body of Christ and his followers too. Please live right and according to his word so, that I too can be free and finally live in peace.

It is so important that we live Holy and stay free, so that the souls of others can in deed be set free. Even as Jesus has delivered it unto us let's be mindful to be ready to freely give it back you see. It is our lives that we must give that others can obtain life and the anointing simply to obtain true peace from within.

It is the will of the father that we not walk selfishly and in our own will, deny others of the yoke breaking anointing that is here to set them free. For there are many souls who have not yet come into the sheep fold who have need to be delivered. Therefore, let us walk in unity loving, supporting, and upholding each other in truth. Let the truth over shadow you and allow Jesus Christ to use you that we all may be free. Remember that I need you and you need me for we are still one body you see. Let us vow to God the father that our lives of love will be found, for those lost souls that are still searching for true deliverance you see.

KEYS TO SALVATION

TRUTH

Always be truthful with Christ No matter what state (meaning no matter what you are experiencing weather it is loneliness, lust, anger or frustration) always tell God what you see operating in you so, that he can deliver you. Keeping in mind that you now have the power to bind and lose. Therefore, whatever you may see don't fear it or run from it just take authority over it. In turn, keeping yourself open to God because he is aware of what's working in you. It's just a point of you remaining honest with yourself and with God.

DETERMINATION

Be determined to stay with Christ. Remember he will never leave you. This takes a made up mind. This means that no matter what you experience in this life (no matter what persecutions may come, trials or storms) you will stay with Jesus. Knowing just what state you were in when you let him in and remembering just how Christ has brought you through. With these things in mind be determined to stay faithful to Jesus. Because after all he is the one who died for you. He gave up all that he had just for you. He was the only one who made the ultimate sacrifice so, that you may gain eternal life. This is his love for you. His love is the only love that will ever see you through Jesus love will carry you through every wave and every strong wind. Jesus love will never end.

BELIEVE

In order to truly begin this race you must first believe IN THE NAME OF JESUS.

Because in his name is relief from life's storms. As you grow, you will begin to operate in spiritual warfare. Your victory is in his name, because, he is the word of God. Your deliverance is in his name. Call on his name. Do not be ashamed of what you see and don't let the enemy deceive you. Jesus' will is true he will see you through.

Written By
Tracy Harris
I. S. B. H. G.

THE GREATEST LOVE

You know that many of us enter into relationships everyday throughout the United States. Believing that our partners love is that enduring, long lasting and never ending love, forgivable enough to weather any storm.

You know that Love that is most capable of holding through unemployment, and abuse. You've seen that Love withstand anger and the storms of jealousy too. We've seen those loves that have continued or endured faith and even a little mis-trust; while conquering everything, the hands of time have sailed on high tossed sea waves your way.

We have proven to be long-suffering with each other. This is one comfort zone that I can lay and rest in ". Then it happens!!! You encounter a sin that unravels every sin. It is so unforgivable that your love has come to an end. The trust that you once had unravels and escapes you. Your hopes of mandible love over takes you. The shame of betrayal well, it consumes you.

However, as you weep and cry Jesus looks from on high. Seeing your heart and drying your eye, with his arms open wide he speaks with a warm piercing cry "In my arms lies forgiveness.

I have seen your mistakes and your sins are not so, great and your sins which are hidden deep within. "Come to me" I will take you in. For my love is great forgiving every sin. My child you may still come in. My peace will soothe you, and my compassion will mend your brokenness. My forgiveness will heal you and my anointing will restore you. For in me lies the greatest love".

DO YOU DARE?

Do you dare to stand by faith; do you dare to seek his face? When all else fails you and all war breaks loose, when trials surround you do you dare? Once every one fails you, with trouble on every side and persecution barking at you will you dare? Can you dare to stand on the truth? When mockery overwhelms you and even the body of Christ begins to doubt you, do you dare? When the enemy curses you and you know that God's word is true can you stand on unshakeable ground?

What a good question! Never wavering after all that you do get, will you dare. Knowing his words are true that if all else fails you his words will catch you. When you begin to question it too will you dare? Will you dare to stand by faith not seeing your great escape? Not seeing the ground or his words that are, so true beneath you? Can you dare to stand by faith that bridge over troubled waters? Again when everyone fails do you dare?

FRIEND

A friend is a counselor, companion, someone to trust, to believe in, to rely on, to depend on, and to confide in. Who has been your friend? On whom do you depend? Jesus has been my friend and on him have I come to depend. Jesus has been a friend on him shall we all depend. Jesus has been my trust of whom the body of Christ must come to trust. Jesus has been my hope and through him must we all cope. Jesus went through the cross. Tell me just how much you lost have. Jesus gave up his life.

Why then can't you be a friend? Since Jesus died on the cross, don't you think that with your life you too must pay the price? Surrender your life to Christ; because, you too must pay the price. The price for your life was paid by Christ. Render your life for the love of Christ. Obey the word and sail in the love of Christ. The wind bloweth and the boat sails over the waters of truth. Allow Jesus to be your friend too.

LIFE

My life in Christ is not all it should be, but I confide in him. You see I don't conceal things. I tell him where I am and he knows me. I confess my faults and he forgives me. I learned to identify my falls in hope of not continuing in them. I believe in the word of truth and I allow it to change me. The truth is what I am and in Christ I have a life. Because my life begins with Christ and in Christ is my life.

Why Lord Why?

So, often we ask the Lord why? So many times we wonder why all of this or why that? Even why me Lord? When in reality it is he who should be asking why? Why haven't you called on my name? When your storm came and the wind blew and the rain fell and the seas roared why haven't you called on my name? When the ground under your feet shook why didn't you run to me and why didn't you call on me (Jesus)? When the trial that I ordained and allowed from the foundation of time came upon you, you ran to man and you stood and walked in your own understanding and not mine. Why did you not seek my face? Why did you not desire my counsel and why ask me why?

I have ordained and allowed all things. There is nothing that is out of my hands. Nothing that is out of control, knowing this and knowing that I have given you peace in my name JESUS. That in my name lies rest. My question to you is how long? How long will you wait to call down the strength that I have given unto you, the love, the peace, the joy and the counsel. Above all how long must I wait to be included in the trial that I have allowed? Therefore, the ultimate question is how long my child must I wait? My name is Jesus.

A Higher Place

A higher place you see. I seek to finally become complete. A higher time I seek a finer line in this time. My heart ponders for that deeper Christ within me. Total growth you see that is the desire that Christ has put deep within me.

I can't shake it there simply must be less of me. I can't change me, but I know that the Christ within me is more than capable you see. Words cannot explain the burning or the groaning that I feel within me.

To look at me you can't see the things I feel only Christ can reveal. I have tried you see, I have tried to change me, but I need that anointing that rich anointing from heaven you see. That good old sweet soul saving, yoke breaking anointing to set me free. That I can soar into higher plains and a different level in Christ you see. Higher heights and a newer flight, that's where I will allow Christ to take me.

ENCOURAGE

Roses are red, violets are blue. Jesus cares and so do you. Trust in The Lord with all your might. Believe in his word for it is light. Know of his ways and pursue his law. For Jesus has brought you through before and he'll bring you through this fight. Tempt not your faith but believe in him.

If you know that he cares then know that he shares in whatever you go through. Your troubles are few because, he cares solely for you. Look to the hills from which cometh your help. Your help is stored in Jesus for he died solely for you. Remember this is a personal race to take it personal is not blue. Believe in the Lord for he knows of you. He sees your hurts and he knows your cares, Just remember he cares for you and this is a joy to embrace through and through.

ANOINTING

The presence of God. The anointing the presence of the king. The peace and glory of our Lord. The block breaker, the ice chipper, the rock crusher, the power of deliverance the anointing. The anointing the comfort keeper, the yoke revealer, the one and only anointing. Who can survive without the anointing? Who can be delivered without the anointing? Who can live in peace without the anointing? The presence of the anointing is, so sweet the peace and the contentment are, so awesome no man can compete.

Anointing, anointing have your way. Anointing, anointing come in today. Let your presence be known before man. Let your sweeping power stand. Breathe on us anointing. Deliver us anointing, speak to us anointing and declare liberty this week.Let every waking day be filled with your presence. Let every precious moment be covered in your comfort. Be still; be still, so that you can feel the anointing as it chills.Be still; be still that that yoke can be destroyed by the power of 'the anointing.

Don't run, but lay hold on your freedom. For the anointing has come to deliver you. Let the anointing set you free, so that you may walk in all of your liberty that Christ has decreed for you I'm free, I'm free the anointing has set me free. I'm free; I'm free now I can walk in my liberty. Liberty, liberty, oh! how sweet is liberty. Liberty, liberty come and taste of this sweet, sweet victory. The anointing oh! how sweet and free it has made me.Come one come all and experience the liberty that Christ has given me through his great sweeping anointing.

A Joyous Season

A joyous season and your love is the season. A season well spent in every event and time is of essence in bad times and pleasant. Through all sorts of weather be it sunshine of feathers or a troubling tornado. Families come and go but you withstand every blow (Jesus). In the heat or in the snow your love stays a float. Expedient and fair your trust never fails. Full of joy and peace you send praise through my teeth.

Full of meekness you see, you keep me complete. No matter the season the love of Christ is always the reason. In trouble or blows Jesus always knows. Thinking of that great sacrifice now that should bring joy to your life. What is my reason you say? Our gracious Father has permitted you to stay complete its true his plan for you in any season. Don't give up your life; because, it will be no great sacrifice. Only through Jesus Christ are you supposed to lose your life. Remember there is a life to gain when you don't live this life in vain.

A great heavens reward is set before heaven's door. Rejoice this night and confess Christ. Give him your life and take upon yourself a greater sacrifice. Holiness you see in this life before Christ well that is the price. As you walk the road of Christ keep in mind that Jesus is the reason no matter what the season. For his life gave you the right to partake of every one of Gods spiritual rights in every season. Jesus is the reason for this joyous season.

TOO GROW

To grow in love and charity too. Peace of mind towards all mankind. Overcoming error and starting a new. Examining our ways in only one truth Burying the lies and walking a new.

To grow is Christ to love is too. To uncover the sin of hidden things releasing the past and forgiving men. To walk in newness not to pretend. Pretending to live only to live in sin. The time has come to grow for Christ.

Put away the pride and release old ties. Begin with him for he will forgive every sin. This is the year to walk in truth. Confess in faith, this year will be a year of growth and produce the fruit of faith that is expected to be pruned each year from the tree of fruit that you expected to grow and produce through life's experiences.

Jesus Is

Jesus is love, growth and peace. Jesus will supply your every need. Jesus is trust, hope and faith with him you can make no mistake. Jesus is endurance and a friend. In him you will lack no peace within. Jesus is fame and in him lays no shame. Jesus will be everything you need. All you have to do is stay on your knees. Jesus is all you will ever need; because, he's the only one who holds the keys.

Jesus is tall and holds the life you need. If ever in sin he'll show you from deep within how to flee. Jesus is all the world ever needs. If they would repent he'll wash them clean. Jesus is the way the truth and the light. His love will bring you spiritual sight. Jesus is here, so please follow him

All you must do is believe. Jesus will never fail. Just don't be a dope and not walk in hope, but believe you can grab hold of his word. Jesus will always be your guide; because, he has his father's eyes.Didn't you read in the word? Don't you know that his eyes travel to and fro beholding just how much you can cope beholding both the good and the evil. Jesus is all you'll ever need, remember all you must do is believe. Remember, Jesus is the very life will ever need.

SOMETHING SPECIAL

Something Special Something Right
Something Special Something Nice
Something Good Something Pure
Something New Just for you

Jesus died on a cross. Something special just for you. Something good, something new Jesus loves you just for you. Something special, something pure give your love he waits for you. Something true, something blue confess your sins he sees' you. Believe in love, believe in truth. Jesus waits just for you.

TODAY

Today is the day of mercy and grace. Today is the day to continue on in this race. To keep the faith and to seek his face, as the day rolls on keep in mind, his love is greater than any storm. Know that this day you have someone of great power at hand. Therefore, guard up your faith my dear saint. For this is not the day to faint. Be strong and call on that great name (Jesus).

There is no problem to great that he cannot make straight. Keep the faith my love, because, Jesus is standing right in front of your storm. Keep the faith my saint roll right on through that storm with a strong hand of faith believing that Jesus Christ will make all things complete.

No matter the confusion Jesus is the problem solver. Be of great faith; because, he is moved by faith. Frantic or frustrated well that two will pass away once you begin to call on the name of Jesus. Don't believe, and you say that you have never truly believed.

This is a start for you Jesus is here to make your life more complete in him. Keep the faith there is still hope no matter what the case your life is no mistake.

For his grace will pave the way today. A new start for all in spite of your past mistakes just calls on his name. By faith watch him make away and behold your faith will soar in your face, because, today is your day.

JESUS IS

Jesus is like fresh morning dew. He is like the beautiful soft sunset resting upon the white clouds. He is like the peace and contentment you'll find seating in a field of flowers. He is like watching the clouds in the sky move and from different shapes while the shadows of your day simply pass away.

When your soul is troubled and you can't rest Jesus is like that water the brings peace and calms all your fears and removes your stress. When you can't find rest in any situation, just call on Jesus. Jesus is like that comfort that you'll find when you're having a one on one talk with your mother.

That reassurance that comes upon you, that peace that consumes you and that ray of love that over shadows you well that is Jesus. Question!! After knowing what Jesus is or can be why haven't you called on him yet?

THE LOVE OF GOD!

The love of God surpasses all of our stupid ways, our mental thought and patterns. He passes right through our plans or our visions. When our imaginations flare up, it brings many things with it that too God passes right through. When we're alone and going through our minds can see our way through, but guess what? He (Jesus) passes through that too. He over looks our anal ways and gives us more credit than what is due. You know as we work ourselves up & down Jesus passes all around. He applies his word and he applies his love that sees us through. The love of God is above us too.

FALLEN

Behold I look and see that pride has taken over me. Pride, pride I must remove it from my side. I see just how it troubled me. Pride should never be my guide. My eyes were blinded you see. I could not see how far I had come from thee. My job, my God I blamed it on my job. My time, my time I did not rightly divide my time. My schooling, my schooling,

I allowed it to trouble me. That's how pride dived right on in. It sought the perfect time to slide on in and hinder me, but thank God for grace. For it was grace that washed my face. It was grace that defeated pride and returned me to my rightful place in this race. Thank God for grace for even though I had fallen I am still in the race.

DEEP

What is the definition of deep?

Deep means extending far from some surface or areas extending far downward: extending well inward from an outer surface. When you say deep think of Jesus. Ask yourself who else would walk with you through the grave yard in your heart? Who else will dig deeper than the surface of a hidden situation that no man can see? Who else will love you when you're at your lowest point spiritually.? Who else will love you in spite of your disobedience? Who else would be here for you when everyone else leaves you standing? When you find yourself slipping, when you're losing your grip, and when you can see the hem of his garment leaving your hands. Who else will be there? JESUS!!!

Saints of God. when you're fighting to give it all over to Jesus, when your struggling to hear the word of God and when your battling to walk the walk and talk the talk, who's deep enough to be there??? JESUS!!! Saints of God I have been there and Jesus is the only one who is deep enough to love me enough through all of this. Jesus is the only one that is deep enough to go through my sink with me. Jesus is the only one deep enough to love me in spite of all of my faults, my sins, and all of my short comings. Saints of God I have found out that Jesus is the only true friend that you could ever have. Even though I haven't come to know him in his fullness as of yet, he has still been there for me. No matter what state or stage I am in spiritually Jesus has proven to me to be the only one deep enough to love me. Saints of God JESUS IS DEEP.

CONFUSED

What to do! What to do! What is the plan? Moving to and fro not knowing where to go. How will I know? There are, so many choices Buddhism, Christian, Jehovah witness oh! What am I to do? Who do I call and what choice do I make? Mother's pulling me here and I have to make a choice. A choice for my life. How do I know and at last just where will I go? For at last I am confused.

"I have an answer". It came in the night and it came by flight. A voice whispered to me late in the night. When all was a sleep and when the day turned tonight. "CALL on his name" it said. Call on his name I said? Whose name I whispered? 'The creator of all things proclaimed the voice Jesus" Jesus I said! Is this a man I thought? 'The creature of all things, the Alpha and Omega the beginning and the end. He will be your friend." As I laid there pondering on that name. I thought well what do I do? Now, there I lay only to say Jesus, Jesus, Jesus please show me the way. Then Jesus replied "I am the truth and the light follow me and I will give you life ". I'll be your friend until the very end. Now you see just how easy it can be. I am free and confusion no longer has a hold over me, because, I am free. JESUS has delivered me.

COMPLETE IN CHRIST

Every year we come to you with new vows, but we never intend to follow through. Every year we claim to trust in you and every year we never really do. And every year we call to you. This year Lord we will be faithful to you. We will allow you to gain honor too. We will learn to climb higher in you. Higher heights and victory in every fight. This year Lord we will truly dedicate more time to you. Being saints of God we must grow in Christ. This is the Year of expectation, inspection of our growth. God examines our fruits this year. Our fruits of labor, love, joy, peace, and trials to see if we have elevated in any area or in what trials. He looks to see just what area or level we have come higher in. Whether it be in temperance or in controlling our anger. He looks to see if we have grown in keeping our peace in finances.

Being able to love and forgive is the greatest of all. Being fruitful in these areas will assure growth in Christ. We must love others even those that are nasty and just downright unbearable with understanding that they are being used by the enemy. Jesus looks for our fruit to ripen and grow every year. This year we start anew. This year we will faithfully follow you in all things complete. We believe your word and our tongues we will hold. With a lot of Christians holding your peace and controlling your anger is a very hard task to do. No matter, if you will surrender both over to Jesus he will take control and your fruits will grow.

Our peace we will keep and our love will grow ever so deep. Our will, will cease while the Christ within awakes from his sleep. We will allow the Christ within to take flight. Again, this year Lord we will seek to be complete in you even babes will submit to you. The struggle they had will cease with you. They too will learn to call to you to allow the Christ in them to take flight. No more excuses will they offer you. No more lies will they tell you. They too will begin to depend on you. Too, trust in your word that growth will follow suit. Denying the flesh and to call on you Jesus. Their will cease and our hearts we give in peace.

BEING SAVED

Being saved is much easier than you think. Being saved is the coolest thing you'll ever see. Jesus saved us and not we ourselves. Jesus will keep us if we would stop and think. It is our thoughts that make this walk impossible 'to keep.

Our will is to please him, but we allow defeat to creep in and it takes the place of faith. Stop and think Jesus is the redeemer and he is also the keeper. Just will everything over to him and our weakness he will keep. While peace and strength he will leave behind allowing us to reach our goal which is eternal life. Be saved for this is truly the coolest thing in deed.

MERCY

What is mercy? Mercy is compassionate and loving kindness. Mercy is sunshine from above with rays of grace shinning down like a dove. Glazing upon the human race with the warmth of loving kindness upon their face. As the son of God stands and beholds the time of man and the souls of old as they grow cold, cold and dead. This is what I have to behold this and all of this is set before man.

Standing there with arms of love and a warm embrace. Waiting to release just a little more grace upon this sinful race. As the time keeps passing right on by his love just gives a deep sorrowful sigh. Looking down from above hoping that his love will change the mind of man and in time hoping to hear a cry aimed above. Hoping this nation will humbly come to serve the only true God and Jesus Christ whom he has sent.

Bowing down on bending knees with pains of sorrow as they come before him and plead "Our sins are great and we would have perished in our sins and this wicked race would have buried us deep within ". Take us in so, that we may be cleansed from our sin and let us take part in the glorious event that is truly meant for every man. To set us free in your liberty no longer having to dwell in this state living so, very blue and suffering in stains, pains and the dispair of man. A greater lift we do seek. Your death was complete for we receive your life that great sacrifice. Because with your love we receive forgiveness and our sins are washed from above. Dear Lord your mercy is adored.

The Love Of Jesus

In the beginning God had one plan and that was to have a relationship with man (spiritually), but since the fall of Adam God set out to redeem man back to him. That all would'nt die in their sins. That's why in St. John3:16 it talks about God sending his only son into the world that we may be saved.

In 1 Timothy 1:15 it speaks of Jesus dying for our sins. In other words he died for you and I. The love of God surpasses all understanding. We could'nt conjure up in our minds the extent of God's love through his son Jesus for us. There are promises of God's devine mercies.

In the book of Lamentations 3:22-23 says that it is the mercies of God that we are not consumed (perish), because of his compassions and how they (mercies)are new every morning. Behold it speaks also of his anger and how it isn't restrained for ever. How if you are willing to repent God will cast your sins into the depth's of the sea in Lamentations 7:18-20.

It is through obedience to the word of God that his mercies carry over unto generation to generations as spoken of in Exdous 34:7. There is mercy in keeping the commands of God as spoken in Exodus 20:6. Jesus learned obedience through the things he suffered. To obtain obedience you must go through some suffering.

In this life you shall suffer if that were not true, Jesus wouldn't have prepared you for it as he did in St. John 16:33. Why not suffer for Christ sake ? Through obedience you will also gain the honor from God. You have so, much to gain from being obedient to the things which you have learned concerining the word of God.

THROUGH TIME

Mercy, grace, guidance, and truth but it abides only in you. Loving kindness, remembrance, and truth Lord knows that it comes only from you. Trusting, truth, learning to only to depend solely on you. Looking thru the eyes of two, I see the goodness of Jesus abiding and shinning through.

The price he paid, for me and you entangled with the love, well seems it came on through. Through time and age, and grace and truth only Jesus is there to help us to come to you. He waited patiently for both me and you, enduring much sin to see us through. The time has come to for you to live in truth.

How much more suffering must he go through before you turn back to truth? How much more time shall you lose? He is waiting it's true in time for you. His only wish is to see you through to eternal glory, this time it's for you, so turn back now return to truth. Because yes! He's waiting only for you. The time is short and the day is too. He's coming soon through time just for you.

PHARISEE

Oh! Pharisee why is it that you think as you think? You walk so, strongly in unbelief. Your unbelief will cause you not to see the truth. Your life is in what you speak dear, dear Pharisee. You are hindered only by what you refuse to believe. Pharisee why do you chose to walk in unbelief?

Christians usually sit and question what the preacher preaches. When you find yourself in this state (it's not that they don't believe; because it is the truth, but simply; because it clashes with their traditions, ways, beliefs, or even culture) you stand as a Pharisee. They refused to receive what Jesus said and preached about in turn they missed out on eternal life.

Stop walking in unbelief and believe all that Jesus has said. Jesus ministered even in their unbelief but, he himself stayed free. The preacher preaches as Jesus gives him (That is those that are sent of the Father not those that sent themselves be careful as to who feeds you). Make sure that they are sent of God appointed and anointed with God's spirit which is the spirit of truth) to preach and teach. The words that you hear are not merely of man you see. They are anointed by the spirit of liberty. Which is Jesus you see. Don't be a Pharisee in unbelief repent and allow Jesus to freely set you free.

WHY HIDE YOUR EMOTIONS?

Emotion, most men are emotional, but do such a great job in hiding their emotions. My question to you is why hide it? Jesus had emotions. The only difference is that he didn't allow his emotions to over ride the word or will of God. Not only did Jesus have emotions, but the disciples had emotions as well. Do you really think that these twelve men and Jesus actually spent 3 1/2 years together without expressing love.

Love means to have affection for denoting personal attachments as a matter of sentiment or feeling. This comes from time spent together, and from an relationship that has developed over the years or simply over time. Both of which had taken place here. You would expect Jesus to be compassionate, because God is a God of compassion and compassion involves feelings. However compassion never hindered God's judgments likewise the same with Jesus.

In St. John 16: 1-15 Jesus explains the events to come with much compassion and discipline. He expresses such emotion and self sacrifice towards his disciples. His love for them is obvious. Why is it then that most men find it hard to express themselves toward their wives? The very ones that they are to give themselves for are the ones of whom they should really be obliged to express themselves with (Ephesians 5:25). Take Jesus he held not back his intent for his feelings.

Likewise were the disciples emotional towards Jesus and each other. Take in St. John l 3:23 where Simon Peter laid in Jesus bosom. Here a grown man express this strong sense of love, comfort and emotion not just to Jesus, but in front of the other fellows. VVhich raises another question why are most men afraid to express their feelings or emotions about their wives or even their love toward each other in front of each other? Clearly the old mentality of the world has been washed away with the cleansing blood of Jesus, and all things including their emotions have been made anew. Therefore, leaving them free to love and express themselves emotionally trusting God in starting a new.

In closing, I only need to say. Look at Jesus his love, mercy, and compassion he expressed openly this is true. Let us do the same for

your wives need the same love and compassion expressed openly to them even as Jesus expressed it openly to you (1 Peter 5:8).Remember that the enemy walketh about as a roaring lion seeking whom he may devour. Even though it is said amongst the Christians that he does not have any teeth. Be sure to remember that he can still swallow a marriage if it is handed to him. Be mindful of (1 Corinthians 7: 3-5). Knowing that Satan only have power if you give it to him.

Look at your wife doesn't she deserve all of your love and affection? Look at her think about the portion of time, care, and love that you have invested in our marriage. Now isn't she and the love you have for her worth holding on to? Be a wise steward over your household. For that wife is from the God of love. Don't hide but, express the gift of love that God has given you.

CHARACTER

The character of a Christian or a person defines who they are and what they stand for. As Christians our character is spelled out for us in Matthew 5:3, "Blessed are the poor in spirit, for theirs is the kingdom of Heaven simply means belssed are the humble-meek in Christ. When the enemy uses someone to oppose you, are you able to agree with your advesary quickly (Matthew 5:25) that you may stay free spiritually? In turn being found guiltless before God or is your pride and flesh in an uproar putting you in sin. Being able to bridle your tongue (James 1: 19) kills your flesh and being slow to speak (James 1: 19) gives you a chance to react with God's wisdom and not with the foolishness of man.

"Blessed are those who mourn for they shall be comforted" Now this means to cry or wale, but Jesus comforts us soley to equip us to comfort others as well as ourselves. We are comforted by the word (2 Thessalonia 2:17). Which speaks of being encouraged thru the word. This is a comfort especially in trying times. This will in turn bring peace to your spirit. Again enabling you to minister liberty to others that they may be free or at the very least be given the option of being free. That's the same choice Jesus gave us in (Acts 9:31) which speaks of the comfort of the Holy Ghost. Which is our middle man or mediator to Jesus.

(Isaiah 40:1-5) speaks of comfort thru deliverance. With every person to have to endure any kind of troubling situation is uncomfortable. When and if found in that situation one usually seeks relief and even deliverance. In (Isaiah 51:1-3) speaks of restoration of joy. Without which, as a Christian it is impossible to minister to someone if you yourself lack joy. You know that the word of God says that "the Joy of the Lord is your strength (Nehamia 8: 10"). Like salvation comfort is not just for us, yet for those that are lost or at the very least, without it and in dire need of it. In most cases they have no ideal of who holds the key to it.

"Blessed are the meek for they shall inherit the earth" Meek symbolizes humbleness and with humbleness comes grace (James 4:6) says that "God resist the proud, but gives rest to the humble." He also guides the humble (Psalms 25:9). Where as in (Psalms 147:6) tells us that" the lord lifts up the humble; he cast the wicked (proud) down to the ground."

"Blessed are those who hunger and thirst for righteousness", speaks of those who desire to live Holy and who desire to learn and grow in Christ. (Luke 1:53) speaks of the hungry being filled and the rich are sent away empty just like the rich ruler in (Mattehw 19:20-22).

"Blessed are the merciful for they obtain mercy. Blessed are those who show mercy (favor) to others for they shall receive it from God and from man. If your walking around being judgemental and not showing mercy to those who have need of it, I would check my spirit and repent if I were you. "Blessed are the pure in heart, for they shall see God. Those who speak the truth and hide not their sins from God and themselves, for the word says that" the true worshiper must worhip him in spirit and in truth. (St. John 4:23)" and (Ps 15:2) speaks of walking up rightly, works of righeteousness, speaking the truth in heart, and no back biting, no reproaching against a friend and no doing evil.

'Blessed are the peacemakers for they shall be called the sons of God. Well Jesus was a peacemaker. He always brought peace between the disciples. Even as we are to bring peace among the body of Christ. If you see a brother or sister in Christ at odds, don't take sides rather get them to look at themselves and not at each other. Remember that Jesus deals with us individually. Allow them to examine yourselves, so that they can see what God has to say about them throught the the word of God. That way they will be able to humble themselves before God and go and apologize to each other, because, God lifts up the humble in spirit.

"Blessed are those who are persecuted for righteousness sake for theirs is the Kingdom of Heaven. Well like wise did Jesus. The beatitudes was Jesus character. We are to take on the same like manor of Christ as he was, so are we now. Allow Jesus to form the fathers character in you even as he displayed it for you. Because as the father is so is Jesus.

THE BOOK

Hay! take a look, take a look at this book. Wow!! it is a book of life and truth. It's amazing just how free Jesus said I could be if only I would believe. Wow!! I can't believe just how sane this life can be. Trials and trouble well they must come, but I have found that my relief and liberty is predestined in Jesus who has come to set all men free. The only thing that could hinder this is unbelief; because belief is the key. The time is late, but you can still escape by his amazing grace. Escape this parshing place and accept your new place in heaven with all the saints. Take the book, believe the book and committ to live for God through the words that he has placed in the book. Learn to serve him in spirit and in truth. Not the letter of the word; because, the letter can not give you that new life in Christ. That new taste of liberty that you need is only found in Jesus on your bending knees through the spirit of the word so, don't be amazed at your new found grace that the Father has given you, simply believe that Jesus can and will.

Everything is based truly on your faith and what you believe God can do. Don't trust in the book but, in the life that is in the book. Because, it is the blood which brought life to us all through Our Saviour Jesus Christ. Please take this book and learn of the life that is required of you by Jesus Christ. Just have faith and believe that Jesus Christ is the only way, and what you truly need. For this is his book and your very life is the greatest sacrifice that is acceptable unto Christ. However, your faith holds the key to your new found liberty. In this book lies the spirit of the truth. Grab hold of this new found life that Christ has taken the time to sacrifice. For it is the spirit of the word that giveth life, so come on and make that great sacrifice and take this book and gain that new life.

WHO DO YOU TRUST?

Trust is to be firm, faithful, and true. Hebrew 10:22 "says let us draw near with a true heart in full assurance of faith, having our hearts sprinkled from an evil conscience and our bodies washed with pure water".

Trust is to be confident or sure. Some of us aren't sure of ourselves, of God or his word. This is reflected in different areas of our lives and evident to others. It could be our families, our friends, or our children. Because, of what we see at times we lack confidence in God's word.

Trust is to be patient, to have hope and it means to wait. What are you waiting on God for? Are you anxious? Are you really waiting on God, or in the back of your mind are you working it out? Philippians 4:1 1 Paul said" not that I speak in respect of wait: for I have learned in whatever state I am there with to be content."

When you are trusting God you are anxious for nothing, but with the state that you are in you become content. That does not mean that you don't desire change. However, you remain in a state of rest until your change comes. Never the less being content, (without murmuring and complaining) in his word knowing that he will come through for you. In doing so, let us govern our conversations as stated in Hebrew 13:5. Because, in trusting God we are to speak what God said and not the opposite. Psalms 118:8 and Prouerbs 3:5 tell us to trust in the Lord and put not our trust in men.

However, I have learned in order to trust in someone you must first be delighted with that person. Delighted means to be pleased with, desire, to be agreeable, to join, to love, to will to desire, and to choose. What do you choose? You choose to will your will to please them. Desire is an intent or longing (you know sometimes our spirit man has an intense longing to fellowship with God) to crave to ask for, or to seek.

2 Chronicles 15:15 talks about Israel's oath and how they sought the Lord with their whole desire and how God gave them rest; with trust comes rest, and no more sleepless nights. Psalms 38:9 and Psalms 73:25 both talk about placing your desires before God. No matter what your desire may be as long as it is according to the will of God. Make sure that it does not go against his word turn it over to Jesus ; because our trust is to be in him. This way we won't seek to fulfill our own desires;because for some it would simply mean walking after our own LUST.

Isaiah 26:9 speaks of our soul delighting in the Lord. When this happens you won't mind those late night's study's, early morning prayers, or those days of fasting;with trust, and delight you begin to commit. Commit means to give to present something. You find that you begin to present your body over to Christ as in Romans 12:1. Keeping in mind that your body includes your thoughts, your will, your emotions, hurts and needs. It involves your whole being.

I Peter 4:19 says that all you commit to Christ he is able to keep. Lets turn it all over to the Lord Jesus; because, in him shall we trust knowing that we can't keep ourselves. In doing, so we will allow Jesus to keep our families, hopes, desires and everything that concerns us. Let us trust.

SLEEP

On fire, water baptised and a living witness! Do you Love the Lord ? Are you prayerful, faithful, fastful, willing to endure trials and willing to love? Have you put aside all malice and unforgiveness. Are you walking in the light? Are you communing with God daily, prospering and witnessing to others? Are you evangelizing the world back to God, and moving in the spirit ever so, fluently?

Then out of no where you find yourself asking what happened? You find yourself becoming tired, too tired to pray. Having more time for carnal affairs than for God. It actually becomes a fight to pray. The battle between the word of God, and your flesh has become intense. Your desire to fellowship has become dull and you can find a thousand reasons on why you should'nt go to church. Well what happened is that you have become relaxed. You have stopped the war. You are no longer fighting, but you are being siffted as wheat. The enemy has made you believe, and feel like you can actually rest. However, this is not true this is not the time to rest. Spiritual warfare is not a seasonal job. You can not join up this month and unlist yourself next month simply; because everything is going good for you. It is your job to stay on top.

Of course the enemy wants to deceive you; because it is his job to undo the damage that you have done in the spiritual rim. It is his job to provide you with a false sense of reality. Because if you sleep then he can work, work, and work. Don't stay in this state. Identify with reality and call upon the name of Jesus. He is the only one who can deliver you from this slumber state. Most importantly, don't desire to stay in this state; because, you stand to lose so much more. You have not even begain to receive the anointing that Jesus wants to release unto you. However, you have to prove yourself trust worthy before he releases any more anointing unto you. Keep in mind that he is watching you with the anointing that he has already given you.

Therefore, awake from your sleep.

REALITY

Sitting here looking through my life. I see my life before Christ, Knowing that he knows the truth. Knowing that if he will I will too. Taking into thought that this life was got by a price. Desiring to know the truth and to abide in truth with you (Jesus). Looking still speaking the truth truly looking thru and thru. Speaking the truth before you (Jesus) and knowing that my love isn't really true and the compassion you see it hasn't completely come thru. You see I am still looking through and I see the naked truth. How about you? Reality what do you see? Do you see the truth? I do, looking through, yet desiring to come into reality with you (Christ).

Knowing that which is not complete shall soon one day become complete. Only through you Christ can reality become true. This is reality that the love of Christ must truly abide in me and you. Not a Holy love but, the agape love that's reality. Search yourself and you will see if the love of God works in deed. I mean look deep within and if you can say that you are complete in the love of Christ without any sin (stains) then you are complete in deed. Remember if he sees it you will too. Reality is life and this life you will only find in Christ. No other God can prepare you to reign with Christ. If you are hiding at home not desiring to really roam with the body of Christ your love will never grow. You can not grow if you do not get into the flow.

Come out of the box and let the love grow in you. You will never love if you never grow no matter what you say. The tiny, tiny dot or particle of love that you share does in no way compare to the reality that Christ is waiting to take flight in your life. This is a time for true reality!

TRIALS

I'm calling my people put from amongest a people" 2 Cor 6:17.

As Christians in this life. There are times when you stop and wonder why others are prospering naturally. Where as with you it seems that your needs are only being met. You feel like something is wrong or unbalanced spiritually. There are thoughts that you can't put into words and feelings you can't explain.

In Pslams 4:3 David (or the writer) tells you that God has set a part him that is Godly for himself, and yet you still ponder at your life, your trials, your victories, your defeats, and your deliverance. You seem to focus more on the most recent trial; because, at this time it seems to have the greatest affect on your life. Now we know that the old testament is a shadow of the things to come. Not once did you think about the children of Isreal. How in the mist of a great nation there was, yet a people called out from a people. How Moses and Aaron were called out from a people.

Part of the children of Isreal resisted temptation and believed God. Where as some died in their sins desiring natural things opposed to things that they could not see. Those that belived not were the ones that made the graven image to worship. However, without those people being called out who would have been there to show or to take a stand for God. For those who belived that it was God who delivered them out of Isreal? Our trials are to make us stronger in Christ, but they are also for a testamoney for others. At a given time in our lifes God will send someone in our paths who are enduring the same trials that we might of just come out of. Simply to be an example or an encouragement to them. Too, let them know that God is no respecter of persons. That just as he brought me out he will bring you out just the same. However, enduring our trials we tend not to think that our present suffering will be a blessing to others. Know that God is real and that he is with us and that through it all we obtain victory through our trials.

Undecided

I sit here and I look. I'm undecided about this book. This book of life and truth. I know the truth, yet I still look. I see my state and I ponder why oh why am I so far from Christ. I find that I have chosen life, but death is here too. It abides within me. You see it abides in the old man this is true. I want to be free to release him from me, but some force deep within just won't set him free from me.

My mind is made up this I can't change. Jesus gave his life for me. I have no one to blame. Away with hell you see. I choose life and that more abundantly. Tonight I die that sinful state that was locked within me. For I have freed that man, that sinful stand. I release him now. To, Christ I belong. Therefore, free yourself, in giving a life you must suffer, but what you lose you shall gain Matthew 10:34

For no man is worth the pain of HELL, so tormenting and sad. Tonight there's life in Christ. Tell Jesus your sins and he'll come in. Just ask him now. If you don't know how, just say I believe you died and raised from the dead. Now come in my Lord I must be saved from sin and death. I must confess I need your love and joy. Oh! boy a peaceful mind I seek to find in Jesus Christ. Tonight I have choosen life. I am no longer undecided. From hell I flee and my heavenly home, well it awaits me.

ARE YOU READY?

Are you ready for Christ? Knowing just where you are now and looking at your life and knowing that Jesus is displeased with sin will you make it in? Realizing that your sins are going to cause death for you even before he comes. Be honest! Look at your life and see yourself through God's eyes. Is he pleased with your life, your ways, your thoughts or your council? By the way I really hope that you are not receiving any council from the ungodly.

Know ye not that your life is wrapped up in the name of Jesus? Do you want to live??If you desire life, just ask Christ to give you life. Confess your sin's and ask him for your life in him. Repent!! accept him as your personal savior. Believe in your heart that he is the son of God and confess with your mouth that God raised him from the dead (this you must first believe), and know that Jesus cares. I mean really cares for you, just trust in him right now. No matter what the situation is, no matter how hard it may seem Jesus can wipe every thing clean.No matter how impossible things may seem know that he will meet every need. Just trust him right now in this very moment.

Listen to your heart (spirit) as it longs for safety, grace, comfort, and peace that it (your spirit) truly desire. Ask now don't wait;because tomorrow just might be too late. Don't try to figure it out. Believe in Jesus. You have tried everything else. You have put your faith and trust in everything and everyone else. All you have to do is trust Jesus he will prove himself to you just believe.

Listen, I know that he will meet every need. For now is the time and the season has come for truth to prevail in your life. You have heard the voice of Christ calling you from your ever so, troubled life. Fall to your knees and confess Christ. Don't give up, be ready for he's here to save you and to meet your ever need. He loves you it's true all you have to do is yield to him. When the Lord ministers to you that is the moment, the time, and the season to surrender to him. Jesus loves you, he died for you, he suffered for you and he's waiting for you won't you come to him now? Are you ready?

I WISH

Son light, son bright the first star I see tonight, I wish I may I wish I might have my life complete in Christ. Son light son bright only to live Holy would be, so right. To please Jesus Christ will be, so nice. Oh! son bright son bright to know that he beholds my life oh, so bright tonight in his sight. Shinning so bright and ever so nice. Jesus Christ is looking at my life tonight. To please him and to seize the right to stand before him ever so right. I wish I may I wish I might have the life that would please Christ tonight.

To live a Holy life ever so, right. To be truthful is the only the only true light. To walk in truth simplified in the love of Christ, well that is truly a son bright. The love of Christ is abroad for us all. It beholds us all with no restraints. Jesus arms are open wide to all. Whether backslidden, troubled, stained in sin, or even weary. STOP! and know that there is a light that is shinning ever so, bright tonight. Jesus Christ is beholding your life within his light.

Believe in his sight that your life can be right before Christ. To know him is to trust him. He will bring you through and he will see you through. Jesus will clean you up and make your life ever so, bright. If only you would submit your life back to Christ. Son light, son bright make your request to Christ tonight.

As Christians we see ourselves, but yet we hide ourselves from ourselves and from others. Our errors, our shame, our pride and even our correctioning. Well Jesus sees right through us (king David said Lord you understand my thoughts a far off). Our complaints etc. Lets face it he sees the real you. Not the person or the anointing that is displayed daily or weekly, but that hidden person or should I say that person that is in the closet. We often hinder ourselves by distorting images of ourselves to others. Instead of noting our areas of weakness, we hide them. We portray such strength and a emotional balance that isn't there at all.

We need to come out of hiding and allow Jesus Christ to be our true identity in truth and in love. Forgiving ourselves first for our errors and praise Jesus for our correctioning. Be strong in the Lord and the power of his might. Not in our image and not in others thoughts, and not in others portrait of us. However, in Jesus strength we can muster our own short comings. To walk in truth is to walk in the open not hiding who we are before Christ. Moreover, accepting who we are and allowing the truth (the word of God) which is Jesus to change us to be free.

THE LOVE OF A CHRISTIAN WOMAN

A Christian woman carries the attributes of a mother. A Christian woman fears God and in turn keeps her house clean (spiritually). A Christian woman takes in her appointed husband given by God, and she treats him with the love and affection she has for her own children.

She is aware of his weakness and attempts to strengthen him spiritually through prayer. She adores his strengths and encourages him. The wife comforts her husband emotionally and watches over him spiritually. Being a creature of affection created by God she learns how to caress him in her arms of comfort. She reassures him of her place with him, and of his place in her heart. This comfort he finds in her only.

A Christian woman is the silent strength of her husband and her house. She holds and caresses him continuing to relax him. To bring him to a place of peace and comfort. This is only done by the love that God has placed in her heart for him. She seeks to please him daily and to display comfort to him each and every day. That he will always come to her for comfort and rest from all that he endures in ministry.

SOMEONE FOR YOU!

I am lonely. I am blue. I am waiting just for you. Looking here, looking there I've grown tired of waiting on you. You say you'll come, you say he'll come, but look here where I sit I'm the only one. I have waited just for him (Jesus). Tell your son tell your daughter that Jesus has someone just for them. Teach them now how to stand, stand, and wait patiently; because, there is someone just for them.Look no more, but trust in him. For the one he'll send is Holy just like him (Jesus). He will love you and he'll be true, simply; because Jesus loves you just for you.

Tell your son how to stand. Teach him to wait for she is coming just for him. One to love him through and through. She'll stand in prayer and fasting too. She'll be faithful and true. She'll make him proud to be his wife, beauty inside and out holiness too. The type of women that Jesus made just for him. Formed in Holiness and shaped in truth, there will be no blues for him.

Tell your daughter this is true no more disrespect for you. Jesus sees and he cares. He has the man who shares.He will send him this is true if only she will be faithful too. She must live Holy this is true.Pure and untouched for Jesus use.Prove yourself Faithful and true to your very first love and he will remember you.Live the life of a tamed wife to the only husband in your life (Jesus).Who has proven himself faithful, trustworthy, patient, loving and caring too. Allow him to keep you true untouched by the devil's flues.

You see Jesus sees you waiting patiently.He knows the truth that's why he has someone just for you.Therefore, let Jesus keep you Holy. Withstand fornication and you can receive that someone just for you, and remember that the best is yet to come. Because Jesus has someone just for you.

ETERNAL LIFE

We know eternal life to be walking in glory amongst the heavenly host, to be singing praise to the Lord. We know of eternal life to be a time of rest from all our trials, tribulations, worries, bills, headaches, persecutions and betrayal. We see eternal life as being an end to our being moneyless, husbandless, childless, homeless, clothe less etc. Overall it's our time to rest from the fleshly fights, a time of complete rest. We no longer have to hear our flesh saying "I don't want to pray, fast or study the word of God" No more rebellious statements towards the word. We see eternal life as malting it to glory, being in the first resurrection Hurrah!!!!!!

(St. John 17: 1-3) Jesus tells us what eternal life is. Jesus said "eternal life is to know the only true God and Jesus Christ whom he has sent" Know means to understand, discern, acknowledge, well known, to be acquainted with, to know thoroughly, honor, to become fully acquainted with. To know God you first must know of his character. Let's examine Jeremiah 9:23-24, here God speaks of relying in the fact that you know and understand him. Not that you are mighty. Which means greatness, strong, brave, army, virtue, and ruler, officer, to be efficient, able, to be active, and to work? This definition alone describes everybody within the body of Christ. Whether you be babes, children, toddlers or adults in Christ.

The word wise means to understand, discern, intelligent, clear sighted, success, or to comprehend. Here Jesus speaks to us all. Rich means to grow, substance and honorable. God also describes himself that we may know of his character. In (Exodus34:6); (Nehemiah 9:17) tells us more about God what he likes and what he is displeased with.

When you know& love someone you want to please them. Jesus did the things that pleased the Father (St. John 8:29), (Matthew 3:17) tell us that God was pleased with Jesus. Jesus was our example. If he obtained eternal life, so must we.

Eternal life is not going to heaven. Going to heaven is the actual fulfillment of Gods promise to us if only we obtain eternal life which is a right now thing. Heaven is our proof of actually knowing God. Acquainted means to Minster to, be serviceable, treasure, requirement and employment. We Minster to God with our lives just as Jesus did. (Hebrew 5:8) tells us that Jesus learned obedience by the things which he suffered. When you buy something it is yours right? I mean you have the receipt of purchase in your hand which states that it is yours. Because we were brought with the blood of Christ we are not our own. But we are the Lords property. Being, so all that we do is simply our reasonable service as stated in (Luke 17:710). Why then do we boast about how we help, give, and lend to others? When it's simply our reasonable service as employees of Christ. We boast about giving when faith without works is dead. Meaning if we see a need and it is in our powers to supply this need and we simply pray leaving the need not meet. This my dear christian is faith without works. We should boast only in the fact that we know and understand God. Therefore, we should watch what we say. Let us Keep in mind that all glory goes to the creator; because, without him we would not be disciplesLet us not be like King Nebuchadnezzar who prided himself in all of Gods works as being his own.

Eternal life is keeping the word. (Matthew 19:17) states that we should not kill our brothers and sisters with our words (James 3:8-12) speaks of blessings and cursing and how it should not be so, amongst the saints. In closing let us obtain eternal life now in Gods righteousness and not ours.

SOMETHING TO THINK ABOUT

As Christians the one thing that Christ requries for us to do is to lose our lives for eternal life (Mark 8:35). Now Jesus had a choice to make when he was in the Garden of Gethsemane he prayed "father, if it be possible, let this cup pass from me; nevertheless, not as I will, but as thou will (Matthew 26:39)." He wanted to keep his life, but in knowing that there was a higher or greater good he gave up his life.

Well what is the higher good for a Christian? Is it salvation, is it heaven or is it honor and favor from the Father through his son Jesus? Something to think about!!! Just as Christ gave his life, yet being mindful of his desire to save his life, likewise, so are we in different situations. However, we save our lives when we compromise the word of God with our desires.

Which in turn shows that we are ashamed of the word; which is Jesus. Jesus said that "who ever is ashamed of me before man I will be ashamed of them before the Father and the angels" That's what we do when we deny the word of God or don't stand in boldness on the word. For example, some Christians are ashamed to tell people that they don't part ;because, they are ashamed to mention why boldly. When in reality others are not ashamed to say that they don't believe in Jesus. Not only that, but the Christian that is ashamed, really want to be accepted by either his fellow peers or his/her family members. That's compromising the truth;because, the word of God say's for us to buy the truth and sell it not. Also Jesus said "know the truth and the truth will make you free."

Our greatest test will be the time of the New World Order. What will you do? Something to think about!!!! A time when we must truly lay down our lives. After becoming adapted with the pleasures of life, the fancy clothes, the nice houses, good cologne, loving family, wealth great health and that's something to think about. However, if we prepare ourselves right now that won't have to be our greatest thought.

PLAY HOUSE

Play house means to pretend to be something or someone that in real life you are not. There are a lot of people infiltrating to be Christian followers of Christ. In doing so they cause a stumbling block to fall on the unsaved; because they look at them and they insist on being who they are and not pretending to play out a role that they cannot play. Not to mention, that they have enough wisdom to know that you don't play with God. Let's play house, well I'll go to church and listen to the word of God without the intent of changing my life and my ways.

I think I'll just go and listen and then I might criticize the preacher who is yielding his life to Christ and oh! Yeah that sister who says that you can't date or even continues to listen to R&B. That mother who says that you must play follows the leader and all of those church folks who say that you can't have any more fun. You know they say that you can't serve God and Satan too. Well guess what I have another thing to show them. I can do my thing and be saved to.

Playing saved isn't hard at all. You know while at church all you have to do is say the same stuff that they say. For example, I'm saved, I'm blessed, or even God is good to me. My favorite saying is God has been so, good to me. You see that's not hard at all. You just learn to mimic what you see.

Eye opener, playing church is a very dangerous game. Your very soul is at stake. If you think for a moment that God is mocked well your wrong. While you were sitting in church you had to have heard this scripture "be not deceived God is not mocked, whatsoever a man soweth that shall he reap." Don't you know that every dot and every word that was preached to you are required to be a doer of it? Don't believe the hype!! There is a hell and if you continue in that same path, you shall bust hell wide open. Don't you know that Jesus died for your sins and by going to hell you make his death and his blood of no effect for you?

Don't you know that he offers you the spirit of truth? Anything that you have to add to your life any substance, I mean to increase your joy or love is only temporal. By that I mean it will only last for a short season, but Jesus is the real thing. He's the real joy, the real peace, the real substance.

Even with food we can only get so, much fulfillment out of that. Then we seek another kind of food. A food that comes from heaven. Guess what, if you're playing house then you never actually get fed; because in order to eat you must take in the food and digest it. In playing house the food is brought to you; however, you never receive the plate and eat the food that God has prepared for you. Therefore, enabling your spirit to really partake of the life that is in the word of God. What a waste!!

What You Believe You Live

BELIEF—is faith truthfulness of God, reliance upon Christ for salvation, assurance, belief and faith.

I believe that a persons beliefs is what identifies them. It is a person's identity or character that people remember. VVhat you believe in you live. Martin Luther King Jr was a black Baptist Preacher. His beliefs and his dream is still remembered by many Americans today. Martin Luther King Jr. believed that Jesus wanted his people all of his people to be free. He believed in the teachings of Christ. Therefore, he lived it.

I believe that was one of the reasons why he was chosen by the believers to represent the Negro race. He represented Holiness, truth, and faith in what he believed in. 1 believe that he was also chosen because, the Negro race wanted the nation to know that Jesus was behind them and that they had a greater power on their side. The same freedom that Mr. Martin Luther King preached is the same freedom (spiritual) that Jesus offers freely to every soul.

A Christian is ready to forgive and be a follower of Christ. As a Christian I believe that life and liberty begins with Jesus Christ. I believe that in Christ lies a spiritual peace, joy, confidence and trust that is yet to be experienced by others.

Being a saved and believing Christian I have seen Jesus through prayer (in Jesus name) heal my mother and bring her from a near death situation. I have seen Jesus shield my 6 year old son from a deadly car accident only to allow him to come out of it with only a simple scar.

I know that living Holy, operating in forgiveness, in love and keeping the teachings of Jesus is real. Like Martin Luther king Jr I to have a dream. That all of Gods people would be free. I believe like Mr. King did so, I to live it. Therefore, my beliefs is who I am.

A MEMORY

I had a memory today. I thought about Jesus and how the disciples fled away. When Judas betrayed him the love that they had well it ran away to. What is a friend? Who has proven to be a friend through and through? Through the good times and the blue? We get hurt, so easily and wounded, so deeply. Yet, Jesus intended on our love carrying on through the hardship.

Don't touches me I'm wounded you see, and being a loner well it has proven to be much easier for me. To be offended over and over is a hard thing for me. To forgive is one thing, but to open up to allow you to hurt me over again well that's just not going to happen. My love is not deep, nor is it shallow you see. I love, but I just can't allow anyone to truly get under my smooth brown skin. This is a hard thing for me. In the former day I would have simply cut you off and wipe away all of the pain, stained tears, and trust away from me with one little swipe you see, for me this was the easy way you see.

Well I have grown some. I will speak to you, and continue on in time not giving any thought to the knife that is hanging from my side. To just ignore it somehow seemed easier than bearing the pain. I mean the hurt of a wound is very painful you see. It is like someone dear to me is standing over me with a knife and they are trying to literally kill me. I mean a person of whom I trusted enough to let them in. A place where very few are allowed to enter there in. This person befriended me enough to let my guards down. You know that great wall of china that we build over time. Well this wall fell down. With no caution at all I allowed the wall to come tumbling down. Trying to walk in complete love. You know the love of God well I was deceived. I believed them to be sincere.

Being hurt can cause a person to turn cold. Therefore, be careful of what you do and say to others. Being mindful that the smallest thing will cause a wound. Let us ask God to set a guard around our mouths and around our hearts. For Jesus said that "from the abundance of the heart the mouth shall speak." Also being mindful that Jesus warns those that offend his little ones and the consequences are deadly indeed.

Also let the wounded be mindful that Jesus loved his disciples and that in spite of Judas' betrayal and the others lack of support upon resurrection he loved them still. In a memory can we see that we too can walk in the full love of Jesus Christ. Tell me just what you do you see? In a memory.

HOLINESS! IT COST YOU

There is one thing that worked in every man whether he is in Christ or not. That one thing is to be liked or accepted by man. One thing that people desire is to have friends and in most cases one friend is acceptable.

To be liked by others makes one feel good about oneself and liked by others. It is something that abides in all man. As a Christian I have come to find that Holiness costs you. That desire to be accepted by man and your peers has a tag on it. You know that in the work place among new individuals you would like to be noticed among your co-workers. You find yourself being friendly which is part of your own character, but what is the price you'll have to pay? In spite of your loneliness you'll have a standard to keep. Holiness! In upholding that standard you find yourself being alone most of the time, because you remind people of their sins and for some you remind them of the vow that they have broken with God. Holiness cost you!!

In spite of the desire to be liked it does not override the desire that God has placed in you to be Holy. Knowing that evil communication corrupts good manners, you find yourself separating from the very same crowd that you once desired to be a part of. In doing so, you have managed to maintain the values, and statues that Jesus has placed in your spirit. However, still desiring to be liked you associate a little, not desiring to be partakers of evil, be it in words or in deed. You can only stay for a very short stay. In keeping yourself you come to discover that you are the talk of the group. They perceive you to be and I quote "HOLIER THAN THOU". Not knowing that you only desire to please Jesus.

However, be careful, because you have Christians who have not come to the point of true holiness. Regardless of the present situation keep in mind that there is nothing or no one that is worth your salvation. Don't be deceived the same God that befriended you, and love you is still there requiring you to be holy. He's the same yesterday, today and forever more. You are to stand through the persecution. Because it is not for you it is simply for Jesus sake. In spite of it all remember that the word of God says "To follow peace with all man and Holiness without which no man shall see the Lord. "Holiness it cost you! Through it all be sure that the love of God and the desire to walk Holy will and does outweigh all other desires. Choose to stand for God always. Your reward is great and worth suffering for, so, goes through with joy knowing that you have pleased the father with your faith. For your reward is eternal life. Holiness cost you!

IN DEATH

Life consists of love, movement, decisions, joy peace and many other important and outstanding things. In life we believe that our body functions extend our life our heart, lungs and our blood and so on. However, it is the breath of life that exceeds our shell. In death there is no movement. In death there is only coldness and great silence. While experiencing death first hand I have come to realize that it is the breath of life that gives us movement, tone, and skin color.

It is the breath of life that allows us to laugh and talk. In short it is the breath of God that gives us life. In (Matthew 27:50) Jesus gave up the Ghost. It doesn't say his heart stopped. The breath that God gives us allows our skin to be soft to the touch and for some it allows our skin to be rough. No matter what the texture of our skin it is the breath of life that allows us to experience this not our shells.

For without the breath of life our shell turns dark and it changes our natural appearance. Our shells represent no life only what we are without life. For our shells resemble an appearance that is really unknown as well as unseen; because you see, an appearance in which you have never seen in life, simply; because, it is death. However, for a Christian it is indeed a sleep and not simply death.

That is if they die not in their sins. In death our shell doesn't represent the life we held while we were living. Remember that in death there is a purpose. Life has a distinctive smell to it. Where as in death there is a stink of no remembrance. Even though for many this life reflects pain, suffering, loneliness, trouble and heart break. Even in these things there is a purpose. In every event we are drawn to God because; only Jesus can heal us. The suffering, pain, shame and heart break is something in which Jesus can relate. Through the rejection Jesus to can relate. In a death you are told to remember only the good times, but that would be a false remembrance; because in life there is good and bad times. For some it is in death that the pain and suffering ends. Remember that in death there is always a reason and Jesus is the only healer.

LIVE IT!

As Christians it is so, easy to speak the word of God and to recite it but, can we live it? (Romans 12: 1) say to present our bodies a living sacrifice Holy and acceptable to God which is our reasonable service. Your body means your thoughts, flesh, legs, ears, arms, mouth, eyes, heart, and every organ there in not to exclude anything.

Every piece fitted jointly together is to be before the Lord in Holiness.

We are so, quick to speak for other's in prayer but, do we discern our own flesh or, are we like the man in (James 1 : 23) who forgot what manor of man he was. We must look at our flesh and confess the sin that is in our flesh unto God that he may forgive us.

Holy means pure, undefiled and clean. This is how our mind and our train of thought are to be clean and pure. Even though we don't we should not entertain the ungodly thought's. The word of God say's that whatsoever things are pure, whatsoever things are clean and whatsoever things are of a good report think on these things.

What's on your mind? Are your thoughts carnal or is there a balance? When I say carnal I mean are you thinking about how cute that guy / girl was or are you thinking about what was said about someone you know or for that matter what was said about someone that you didn't know? What's on your mind? Are you worried about your gas bill or any bill in particular? Are you pondering on just how you are going to make it? Finally is your mind on what Jesus said about every situation? Because you know for everything that we encounter Jesus has already addressed it.

Your body is complete with vital living organs. Which are sensitive to many unnatural things and for some, some natural things? My question to you is what are you feeding it? Know that through your body God use's you. If you are mistreating your body with sweets, pop, sugar, butter, fatty foods, smokes of any sort (Don't try to single or cancel out anything I want you to look at every and all kinds of smokes. Rather it is crack cocaine, let's be real cannabis, heroin, cigars, chewing tobacco, even the smoking pipe. We can't leave out fifty one's now can we? Lack of water, fast foods and greasy foods and salt. Now greasy foods cause weight gain and heart attacks, sweets cause diabetes;while salt cause high blood pressure.

Be advised that you are not presenting your bodies Holy before God. You are responsible for your health. It is your job to maintain it. If Jesus provided the way then we are to walk in the path that has been paved for us. Think about it did you ever hear or see in the word of God about Jesus being in poor health?

Did you ever hear of him being dizzy, because of high blood pressure? Did you ever hear of him having a stroke? I think not because he was too occupied with presenting his temple/body Holy before his Father. Don't you know that sickness is a hindrance unto you and the move of God through you? Transform means similar, resemble, or like. Neither the Church nor the body individually are to look like the world in anyway, form, or fashion. Whether it is in song, dance or music.

Be advised that the church is not supposed to resemble the world in attire, or behavior. STOP that does not mean that we are not suppose to look good, but please by all means do it in moderation. What do you mean moderation? What I mean is this, carry yourself as holy vessels that are owned by a Holy God. When the world see you they see the light of the world shinning through those sharp clothes. By all means don't let the clothes make or break your character. Of which I do so, hope that you are made and shaped with the character of Christ and not of the flesh and the old man.

For this very reason, so many turn from the church. The word of God says that the wife is not to draw people to her simply because of her beauty, attire, or hair, but; because of her conversation which is supposed to be a hOLY conversation (I Peter 3: 1-4). Not one of gossip, mischief, confusion and bitterness. This only brings shame to your head not to mention hardship. For the people will either leave the church or join in the mess. Remember to can't walk together except they agree it's the word. We are not to change to fit the world;because, the world grows worse and worse by every moving second.

We are to take a stand in holiness. People are to be drawn to you by the spirit of God which is in you; because, of the life that you live. Your prayer life, you're fasting, and seeking God and your studying the word of God are the reasons that should draw souls. Let us not conform our ways to suite or please the world even our love ones. For how else can they be saved except they witness the change that Jesus has made in your life? Therefore you must live it.

How Could I?

Life is filled with ups, downs and disappointments all around. The sweet taste of victory is what makes things, so complete. Traveling from day to day knowing what will soon come my way. I am blessed to experience Christ face to face in this life. The joys of salvation and the pains of sorrow that float, so lightly into my tomorrows. Bringing storms of rain to discourage me from this race. How could I make it without his grace?

The pains and agony of these trials today have come to wipe the smile from my face and to fill me with grief and anger. With hopes of burying me, so deep in a grave of pity that stinks. Oh! then there's the sound of laughter. A joy that is buried deep within way beneath my smooth brown skin. It is a secret key for defeat that Christ has given me.

Victory is complete as long as there is strength. Strength will help me to overcome the sorrows of life that I may continue on with Christ. Christ is the key and life is complete when he leads. How could I be complete without Jesus being the captain to guide me through every sea? How could I be complete without his joy that is able to carry me over the stormy seas unto the land of victory? With Christ life is complete ;because, it is his joy that aids me into every victory. Without Christ this life would be a very dark cloud with no hope of ever truly obtaining victory. Every wind that blows and every wave of the sea that seeks to carry me away into its very own misery, I continue on in the ship of peace that my Lord has given unto me. In spite of the waves of the sea, I still sink deeper in Christ who leads me.

Knowing that with Christ the winds will never truly over throw me. As I press through the winds and weather every storm I know that this flight would not have taken flight without Christ guiding me by his light.

Therefore, I say that I couldn't, I couldn't go on without Christ weathering every storm. How can you?

LIFE

(Genesis 2:7) The beginning to man's life. "And the Lord God formed man of the dust of the ground and breathed into his nostrils. Adam was given life but, most importantly he was given eternal life with that same breath. (John 17:3) And this is Life eternal, that they might know the only true God, and Jesus Christ whom thou hast sent.

Eternal life is the life that holds a true balance or weight in the life of man.

Here to know God means eternal life. Know means honor, obey, work, employed if you know God your will should be able to do his will. (John 3:34) Jesus saith unto them, my meat is to do the will of him that sent me, and to finish his work. Jesus spoke of his meat. Meat means pleasure, or vitality. What is your meat?

Whether you are a believer or not. The will of the Father is that all be saved, that all believe in him / his word, that non perish, and that all inherit eternal life. His desire is that all rain with him. Will means purpose, plan, decision, desire, delight, wish, Iodndness, decree, and to intend. Everybody says that they know God. I mean everybody sinners, Jehova Witness, Muslims, Catholics, Prisoners, everybody.

Religious sinners. Oh yeah we have those to. Religious sinners are those who have accepted Christ as their personal savior but, they sin willingly. (Proverbs 8:33-35) Says hear instructions, and be wise, and refuse it not. Blessed is them that hearth me, watching daily at my gates, waiting at the post of my doors. For whoso findeth me findeth life, and shall obtain favor of the Lord.

What I mean is that they premeditate their sins. They plan it out step by step, and moment by moment. With justifiable excuse or reason. They allow their human reasoning to dictate to them. They turn it all over to their will, but they hold fast that confession that they know God. (Proverbs 15:24) The way of life is above to the wise that he may depart from hell beneath.

What is the will of the Father?

Better yet what is your will? (James 1:15) Then when lust hath conceived, it bringeth forth sin and sin, when it is finished, bringeth forth death. Abraham's will was to please the Father. The will of the flesh is lust. James said that when lust hath conceived it bringeth forth sin, let's continue to establish life. (John 6:43-48) Jesus therefore answered and said unto them, murmur not among yourselves. No man can come to me, except the Father draw him: and I will raise him up at the last day. (Talking about the resurrection).

It is written in the Prophets and they shall be all taught of God. Everyman therefore, that hath heard, and hath learned of the Father, cometh unto me. Not that anyman hath seen the Father, save he which is of God, he hath seen the Father. Verily, Verily, I say unto you, he that beheveth on me hath everlasting life. "I am the bread of life".

(Deuteronomy 30:15-20)

See, "I have set before thee this day life and good and death and evil; In that I command thee this day to love the Lord thy God, to walk in his ways, and to keep his commandments and his statues, and his judgments, that thou mayest live and multiply, and the Lord thy God shall bless thee in the land whither thou goest to possess it. But if thine heart turn away, so that thou wilt not hear, but shalt be drawn away, and worship other gods and serve them; I denounce unto you this day, that ye shall surely perish. And that ye shall not prolong your days upon the land; whither thou passes over Jordan to go to possess it. I call heaven and earth to record this day against you, that I have set before you life and death, blessing and cursing: therefore choose Life, that both thou and thy seed may live." That thou mayest love the Lord thy God, and that thou mayest obey his voice, and that thou mayest cleave unto him: For he is thy Life, and the length of thy days: that thou mayest dwell in the land which the Lord swore unto thy Fathers, to Abraham, to Issac, and to Jacob to give them.

Yes he's talking to the children of Israel who were natural Jews. His chosen people but, we are his wild olive branch drafted in by his grace. However, this commandment of life and obedience is for the New Covenant (Spiritual Jews who you are). (John 13:4) "A New Commandment I give unto you, That ye love one another; as I have loved you, that ye also love one another.

If you obey and love—not hate.(Matthew 6:14) For if ye forgive men of their trespasses, your heavenly Father will also forgive you: Forgive and not hold grudges.(John 3:15) That whosoever believeth in him should not perish, but have eternal life. Believe then you shall obtain the blessings of God but, most importantly life eternal.

(John 14:6) Jesus said I am the way the truth and the Life: no man cometh unto the Father but by me.Jesus is the way, the truth, and the light.(John 11:25) Jesus said, I am the resurrection, and the Life: he that believeth in me, though he were dead, yet shall he live."

(Matthew 28:18) And Jesus came and spoke unto them, saying, "All power is given unto me in heaven and in earth." All power was given unto him.

(John 3:16) "For God so loved the world that he gave his only son, that whosoever believeth in him should not perish, but have everlasting Life." Life is in Jesus.(John 6:47) He is everlasting life. Your flesh can be a god. Anything that you place before God is a sin as idolatry.

When you will do the will of the flesh instead of the will of God that is idolatry. If you want to live you must believe in Jesus; because through him is life eternal. You must continue to believe, not a moment of religious belief. Which means you believe solely out of convincing, but a life time of belief. Not an elapse of belief; because, you need him to be a right now God. What is the security you have prepared to leave your family? Is it money or is it peace of mind that as your shell rest your spirit shall be heaven bound?

Why would you want to leave your kids with the knowledge that you are going to hell? What is the extent of your love for them and for yourself. Insurance will only last for a short while. However, soul insurance brings forth peace of mind. Now I ask you, which is greater? Would you like to leave behind a legacy of salvation of financial wealth?

(Matthew 6:26) With a salvation legacy your kids / your kids even down to the third and fourth generation. Will have something substantial to hold on to even in this life. For they will have Jesus. "What profit a man to gain the whole world and lose his soul." Peace is in Christ. After your family has finished fighting over whatever gain you have left behind. Just what will they have to comfort them.Don't lose your soul. Today God has placed before you life and death. Please choose life. For your life is only in Christ Jesus.

WHAT FOUNDATION
HAVE YOU LAID?

(Ps. 4:1-3) Godly! Before anybody can become Godly they must first have a foundation of Godliness to follow. A teacher if you will some form or sort of guidance. A map to follow. (I Cor. 3:11) For other foundation can no man lay than that is laid? This is Jesus Christ. Here Paul lets us know that anything else is not really a foundation; because, a foundation is solid, sturdy, reliable, and dependable. He didn't say that some have not tried or will not try to lay their own ground work. This is because they can't accept truth which brings forth a change.

And it is a known fact that flesh doesn't like change. Flesh rebels and run from change, especially the raw truth. (Eph. 4: 11) Here we have Christ's Foundation for the body of Christ. You see there's an order to everything. Everything must be decently and in order. The world has an order or a system in which it is governed by, well how much more should the church have an order. Here Paul tells us that God gave some Apostles, Prophets, Evangelists, Pastors, and Teachers. Where as in (1 Cor. 12:28) Paul tells us that God has set in the church Apostles, Prophets, Teachers, Miracles, Gift of hearings, Helps, Governments and Diversity of tongues.

Well you might say that they both are the same but they're not. (Eph. 4: 11) say that God gave and gave means to add, put and appoint. Whereas (1 Cor. 12:28) says that God set in the church and set means to arrange, ordained, to put in order, join, and appoint. For there to be a foundation there first has to be a form, a fashion, or a molded shape to follow. Don't you know that God knows man? Don't you think that he knows that if he left him with too much room that he would lay himself in pride, and destruction self righteousness? Here God is simply saying

I have given you a foundation but I have added a little more to it Just as Jesus did.

He kept the law but, nevertheless, he added something in the process. (St. John 13:34&35) a new commandment. (Matthew 5:38-48) (2 Tim 2:19) Nevertheless the Foundation of God stands sure, having this seal. The Lord knoweth them that are his. And let everyone that nameth the name of Christ depart from iniquity. The seal is a life of righteousness. This is so; because, of the life that Jesus lead. He was (1 Cor. 1 2:28). Let's talk about the order of things. God placed the Apostles first.

The Apostle is a commissioner of Christ, a ambassador of the gospel, officially a commissioner of Christ (Apostle with miraculous powers), apostle the messenger, he that is sent. Prophet one speaks forth or openly" a proclaimer of a divine message," denoted among the Greeks an interpreter of the oracles of the Gods.(1 Samuel 9:9) Indicating that the Prophet was one who had immediate intercourse with God. Nabhi meaning either one in whom the message from God springs forth or one to whom anything is secretly communicated.

Hence, in general the Prophet was one upon whom the spirit of God rested.(Numbers 11:17-29) one, to whom and through whom God speaks. What is the purpose of the Prophet according to the order that God set the church in. Prophet inspired man to speak by inspiration. One who speaks forth or openly" a proclaimer". Teacher means to understand, direct, discern, inform, know, and teach. Helps means to aid or relieve, assistance, and assist in the sense of servant. Pastor means to tend a flock or pastor it. Evangelist means preacher of the gospel. However, after knowing, reading, and hearing why then is it that some try to lay carnal foundations. A Foundation that is based on television with a 5 minute prayer? A Foundation of emphasis, boredom, sleep and tiredness. A Foundation based on deceit, foolishness, unstableness, trickery, blindness, mans opinion and ways? A carnal foundation of gossip. A Foundation that is subject to change. A Foundation of worry, and stress. Sometimes people can become accustom to living with these factors and build their lives around them.

A carnal foundation is unstable, and unsound. It moves when it rains. It is weak and unable to hold the structure of a house. Jesus said in (Mark 2:21 &22). This is in reference to salvation. What he is saying is look all that is old or all that you were identified by put it away, because what you have is new and the old cannot contain the new. Likewise with the foundations. Why then if given a spiritual foundation you try to build or place it over the old where even Jesus said it cannot be so. A Religious Foundation is based upon knowing the word of God, but never becoming a doer of the word of God. To become a doer of the word means to display "Faith".

You believe what is said and you do it. This symbolizes faith and works. A Religious Foundation However means that you know what the word says and yet you yourself allow yourself to fall into tempting and uncalled for situations. For example partaking of another's man's evil. A Foundation represents the beginning. A Religious spirit will cause you to be sealed in fornication, lying, denial, pride, self righteousness, and blindness and still confess Christ walking before the Gentiles bringing open shame & disgrace to the name of Christ. Another Foundation is Religious Foundation. Also flesh wants to hear garbage not the spirit man. Once a spiritual foundation is laid the spirit man would rather run from confusion, and gossip, it does not want to hear it. I used to wonder why no one would call me or why I never know what was happening.

However, once I realized just how peaceful my spirit was, because it wasn't weighed down by junk rejoiced. Having a religious foundation means that you walk as the Pharisees. You see yourself in righteousness only it's not Jesus righteousness but it's your own and we know that our righteousness is as filthy rags. The Pharisees kept the letter of the word to the dot, but they never came to obtain the life of the word which is the spirit.

With a religious foundation you never really grow or excel to that level that is required of you by Christ. Instead you walk this life in blindness (spiritual blindness). Always seeing yourself just right before Christ. Never able to receive the truth and surrounded by pride on every side. Foundation!! Let's set aside our foundations of flesh solely to obtain the true foundation of Christ so, that we may obtain eternal life with Christ. (Ps. 24:1-3). (Ps. 15:1-5 1:3) means that you don't lie to yourself about who you are in Christ and you stand spiritually on what needs changing, and what your short comings are and whether or not you need to grow.

You must live holy and work Christ's righteousness and not your own. For our righteous is as filthy as rags. In (Psalms 1:3) "doeth evil" he means that you want try to sneak and try to do a thing believing to walk in righteousness. You know we will say the word, but do we see that our spirit is foul in the process of a deed that we may be doing to our neighbor. Let's first establish that our neighbor is our comrade, kindred man, another fellow neighbor any of kind (Them that come nigh at hand, brother, lover, friend, husband, one another a fellow citizen inhabitant close by, or near).

PEACE

Peace how sweet is the serenity of peace. The calmness and the silence of peace. The sound of no one calling your name. The rest in knowing that this time in space is only for you. How precious is this moment. The sound of silence and the moment of emptiness. There is only one place that you can find this rest. There is only one who can give you this rest. Oh!! how wonderful it is to not here the sound of pithier patter feet.

The rest of motherhood and the not so often opportunity of not having to meet any needs. The soothing sound of silence and sovereignty in the back ground. There is only one time in space and only one time according to your faith that you can find this peace in this place. JESUS is the only one who can provide this peace for our human race. Money, drugs, men, friends, family, and not even sin is able to provide this priceless thing. If you would only come to Christ I'm here to tell you that your life will be so, complete. Because Jesus is the only one who is able to meet your every need. Ril you must do is pray and believe. Believe that he can and that he will, but most of all you must pray in Jesus name.

SOLIDER AT ARMS

My Solider at arms, always ready to fight. Dedicated and committed you have fought a good fight. Like David my name is your weapon of choice. But often the hurt, and despair within your spirit enters my ears as a praise of heavenly host exalting my name, and giving me reverence. Those who oppose you stand wondering "why is he behaving like that? No weapons of flesh that can't be right? Even he must react unfittingly because of this and that."

You are Judah my solider of war. Your praise has caused your enemy's to find safety in me; while your praise and your forgiveness has caused my mercy to cover your enemies. My solider, My David, my son you sent my word out like a boomerang and it accomplishing just that deliverance not vengeance. I'm please that you know where my heart is at.

My unique solider, your army awaits you at my feet. Not yet, but soon my son. soon you will lead many and I will silence the nay sayers that say" Why, haven't, and didn't you come to remain with us?"

My call and my purpose are before you. You stood in peace. You Instructed many in my name; while you Dared to Love those whose shame the enemy desired to spread like fame.

You have enlisted many in my name. You have danced and praised in my camp in my name. Endurance drips like sweat from your face while tears of love cover everyone's mistakes. Your life has been a reverence unto me both natural and spiritual births have been declared in my name. **Jesus** is the only fame you have declared.

I see you standing with my armor on as proof that this battle has been Ordained by me. My Prophet, My Preacher, My warrior My son you are my **SOLIDER** at arms.

Written By
Tracy Harris I.B.H.G

WHAT'S WORKING IN YOU?

(James 1: 13) talks about being tempted and how you are not tempted of God. To many of us think this scripture reflects on adultery and fornication, but there are many temptations that test and try us. God is not the tempter because tests bring forth sin that is either doormat or living deep within. Test and temptations show us what's working in us so, that we could go before Jesus and ask him to deliver us. That we can see what God already sees. God allows the enemy to come against us, or should I say that God allows the enemy to test us. Even better than that God allows us to go through test and trials to work out the hidden sins and transgressions that abide in our hearts.

Let's look at (Luke 8:10-15) Jesus talks about the different seeds and the grounds that the seeds fall on.(Luke 8:12) talks about the way side seed. Now this seed speaks of a certain trial that you endure over and over or at the very least one that you are currently enduring. The way side seed is that you go to church already experiencing trouble (a trial). You hear the word of God and rejoice, but later the same trial returns because you never passed it.

The word was stolen from you. How do you know this? Because whenever you have a trial and you don't pass it guess what that same trial returns again giving you another chance to pass it. But because you have forgotten what you have just heard in church you failed the trial. Sometimes God will send you a word to encourage you while you're going through trials and tribulations, but this word also comes with instructions. However, because we are emotional we rejoice during the word (rejoicing because God really cares about what we are going through and to know that we are not necessarily wrong we rejoice) by the time that the service is over we are going through a conformation period with other saints, of whom we have shared a part of our tribulations with.

That we forget the word allowing the enemy to come in and take it. By the time that the trial is over that's when we remember the word and that's when we realize that we have failed the exact same trial that God just gave us a way out of. For many of us this is a temptation depending on the type of trial that we are enduring (James 1: 19-27).

Not only do we forget, but we also forget the word of God, but we forget what's working in us as well. During most of our trials it is our smart mouth, a sarcastic spirit, and a spirit of anger that gets us in trouble. Flesh causes you to be spotted and for most of us anger causes us sin. Because, we sometimes refuse to agree with our adversary quickly as in (Matthew 5:25). Now this does not mean that we are wrong, but what it does allow is for you to humble ourselfs and hold our peace which in turn gives God a chance to fight our battles for us.

Next we will talk about the seeds that fall on the rock. Now this parable talks about the seeds that fall and they grow, but because beneath the soil or a level deeper than the top layer or cover there are some issues or hindrances which hinder that seed from reaching its full potential in Christ and in growth. Which causes the seed to wither away or not so much the seed but the productivity of the Christian to be stunted. There, is a natural reason for this the word root means mental action or activity, to become stable. Whereas stable means to set up, establish, fix, prepare, stand, faithfulness, and order. Let's deal with faithfulness many people are not stable;because, they cannot be faithful to Jesus in any way.

They start one thing and without finishing it they start something else. Another area of unfaithfulness is identified in prayer and time with God. This will cause a person to not be faithful to God concerning spiritual matters. Another example is if you start building a house and lay the foundation then you leave that project simply to go and start another one. This is considered unstableness or Double mindedness.

Your salvation requires faithfulness and time and commitment. When you started building this house you cannot suddenly stop and start another function. You must finish what you have started. Especially when you are building something. Building a house involves mental action or activity. Likewise does your salvation involve the same thing? Salvation is more than just words. It is action, action in prayer (which means that you must pray).

Even if you start out with just a few words. Know that in time God will turn those few words in to many as you continue to build in faith. You do this by establishing faithfulness in prayer or a prayer life. In doing this you will begin to pray the word of God which equals action, action in faith. Because the more you speak it the more you are likely to believe it, receive it, and walk in it. This will cause you to establish growth and to become rooted in the word of God.

Order is another part of being rooted in the word of God. A lot of people are not stable because their lives are out of order. For example, during my first year of marriage my mouth kept me in sin, the sin of disobedience. My husband would speak a thing and; because I didn't agree with him, I would run my mouth. He would ask me to be quiet, but; because I was not rooted in the word I could not obey him. I continued to fail this trail for more than one reason. One of these reasons was because I didn't have or understand the word or even observe my life, action, or even my reaction to the word of God. Not to mention the fact that I didn't examine myself. Leaving me a prime example of (James 1: 19-27). In order for your life in Christ to be stable, and rooted you must first be in compliance to the word of God.

Last, but not least, we have the word or the seeds that was choked by the cares of this life. I believe this scripture is self explanatory. They hear the word, they believe the word and they even live the word of God. But their desires (the things that they want or even the things that they desire to accomplish, begin to choke the word of life that has taken root in their lives. Cares and the riches choke the word of life. The cares can be a family member; because many of our family member's remain unsaved after we have taken that awesome step into eternal life. The things that we see, and hear can try our faith in God's word which in some cases will cause unbelief to grow and choke the word of faith that was established in our lives.

Another is riches now in riches we can allow the blessings of God that were spoken to overtake us. How do they over take us you say? They over take us by replacing prayer, fasting, bible study, separation etc. Which in turn causes us or the word in us to begin to die. I don't believe that you say. Well let me explain it to you. Let's look at a tomato seed. When you plant that seed you take it and you bury it into the ground.

Now being a good planter or farmer you have done your research and you have found that this soil is good, so you continue to plant the seed. After doing that you begin to water the seed and make sure that the seed receives enough photosynthesis; which is needed for all plants to grow (sunshine). Now being a good farmer you watch over your investment and you see to it that it grows. If you were to stop feeding that plant after its growth and took the sunshine from it, the plant would die.

Well the same thing will happen to you. You still ask why? Because when we begin to seek or even put more or all of our time into cares, riches, and desires we find that we don't have time for God. Where at the time that we had put into prayer we no longer have that time. Even the time that we put into bible study (which is supposed to be our mind feedings) in our minds we have better or more important things to attend to.

Whereas there was one time in our lives that we truly found these spiritual things to be of greater importance to us, but look at us now can you see these things choking the life of Christ out of us. These are the temptations that we are faced with everyday, but in Jesus name we shall overcome each and every one of them and maintain our lives in Christ. Being rooted and grounded in him that is the key.

CHECK YOUR HEART

(1 Samuel 15:1) Verse 5 Here Saul warns the Kenites and he has great confidence in obeying God. Hear we have Saul & Samuel. The instructions of God have been given to Saul. He starts out with the mind & will to please God. He gathered the troops spared the Kenites and went to the battle, but what happened? What reasoning went forth that made him spare the King of the Amalek a gag?

Check Your Heart. (I Samuel 15:5) You see as a warrior he had to straightly pick the right moment to strike (just like our army U. S. before they enter battle they study their enemy and peek out their weakness). Well not being prepared for a battle proved to be the Amaleks weakness. So he laid their & he watched them. He watched them long enough to warn the innocent by standers. Verse 7 he gave the signal and he smote them. How it said that he smote them from Havilah until shur which is against Egypt.

That means that they ran and Israel had to travel some distance to catch them and kill them. Look at the effort that they put into their battle. I can see them on their horses. Knee deep in battle, but something happened in Sauls mind. Human reasoning. It shifted from obedience to human reasoning. Some where within that time his will shifted. What human reasoning caused him to detour from the will and the instructions of God? What human reasoning has caused you not to obey the voice or will of God? How did you rationalize to yourself on why you shouldn't witness to that girl or why you didn't pay your bill?

Human reasoning can really cause you to walk in error towards the will & plan of God. Verse 9 of Chapter 15 says that Saul & the people, keep the best of the sheep, oxen and the fatlings. Now that displays Unity in disobedience. You see two people can't walk together except they agree. Saul being the King, the head and the ruler simply reinforces what was said of old, that if the head be sick then the whole body is sick. What was at work in the heart of Saul just spilled over unto the children of Isreal. Because he had already given them the instructions of God to follow, however he himself had disobedience at work in his heart. Therefore, in not standing in obedience he took everyone into sin. That's why if you are a leader or over anyone or even if you are recognized as some sort of a leader it is essential that you examine your heart. Search yourself and allow God free will to do likewise.

Look at yourself, look at your ways and most of all listen to yourself as well as your thoughts. How else will you really know what's at work in your own members? Let us not blame everything on the devil. Come on lets face it, some of those thoughts are really yours. The key to salvation is truthfulness first to God and then to yourself. OK lets bring it home.

If you confess Christ as your Lord & Saviour examine yourself because you can cause people to stay in sin (By being a hinderance with the wrong attitude, behavior or even with the wrong response. Lets face it, people are just looking for a reason not to follow Christ) or even to sin; because, of your actions, or even your speech examine yourselves (heart).

Saul didn't examine himself until it was too late. It says that they took the best of the fatlings, oxen, and sheep this also represents lust of the eye. They keep all that looked good unto them. Everything that looks good isn't good for you. Ask King David for he looked upon Bathsheba. Now we all know that that wasn't good for him spiritually, because that cost him and his families peace. Overall when you don't examine yourself first you can become blinded instantly.

Learn to start counting the cost. Examine where your actions will take you spiritually and the repercussions of both your action and your speech will have on others as well as yourself (along with your walk with God). Because Saul had great confidence in obeying the instructions of God in verse 5. But, if you read on you will see that the disobedience &

the lust of the eye were just attributes of the root of the real issue which was a man pleasing spirit (Verse 24 Chapter 15). Even I after reading just how quickly Saul sinned against God had to examine myself.

Even in his blindness he still believed himself didn't he? Saul wasn't King for just one night or even for aweek, but whatever the length of time, see how quickly he was turned against the voice of God to please the people. As Christians we must be careful as well as watchful. When it comes down to darkness, those of the light (Because even Christians, Saints, or whatever name some are named by will attempt to influences you the wrong way.

Remember that their are tares amongst us too), and some who occupy both a taste of light and a shade of darkness in them.

Keep in mind that the enemy will use whom ever is available to pull you out of the word or will of God. For Saul it was the children of Isreal. As leaders we must be strong and determine to stand on the word of God incomplete obedience. Let's keep a clean heart so, that we may abide in God's tabernacle (Ps. 1-2). Counting the cost of our actions even as we had to count the cost of salvation. What I mean is taking in account what it would cost you to build your spiritual house of salvation (your life and what you had to lose to gain Life). Lets do the same for others by watching our heart.

Printed in the United States
by Baker & Taylor Publisher Services